NATURE SPY

NATURE SPY

written by SHELLEY ROTNER and KEN KREISLER
photographs by SHELLEY ROTNER

SCHOLASTIC INC.

New York Toronto London Auckland Sydney

Text copyright © 1992 by Shelley Rotner and Ken Kreisler.
Illustrations copyright © 1992 by Shelley Rotner.
All rights reserved. Published by Scholastic Inc., 555 Broadway,
New York, NY 10012, by arrangement with Simon & Schuster
Children's Publishing Division.
Printed in the U.S.A.
ISBN 0-590-67828-0

5   6   7   8   9   10   11   12   08   08   07   06   05   04

For Emily, my little nature spy
—S. R.

For Linda, dream a little dream with me
—K. K.

I like to go outside—to look around and discover things.

To take a really close look, even closer

and closer.

My mother says I'm a curious kid. She calls me a nature spy.

Sometimes I look so closely, I can see the lines on a shiny green leaf,

or one small acorn on a branch,

or seeds in a pod.

I notice the feathers of a bird,

or the golden eye of a frog.

When you look closely, things look so different—
like the bark of a tree or an empty hornet's nest,

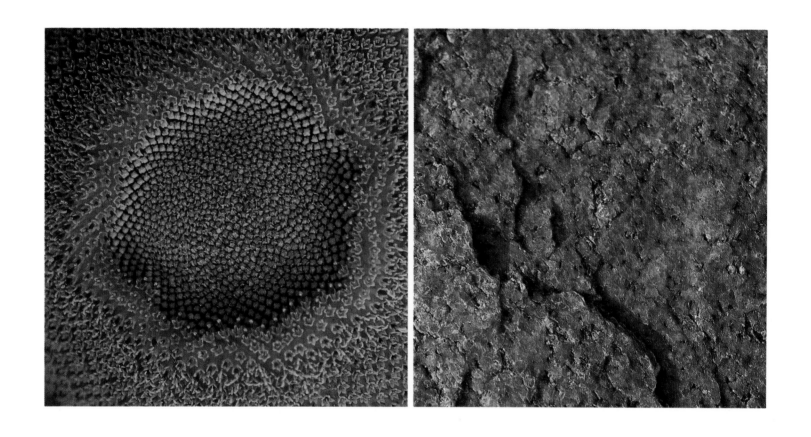

the seeds of a sunflower, or even a rock.

Sometimes there's a pattern, like ice on a frozen pond,

or a spider's web, or a butterfly's wing.

Everything has its own shape, color,

and size.

Look closely at a turtle's shell,

23

or a dog's fur,

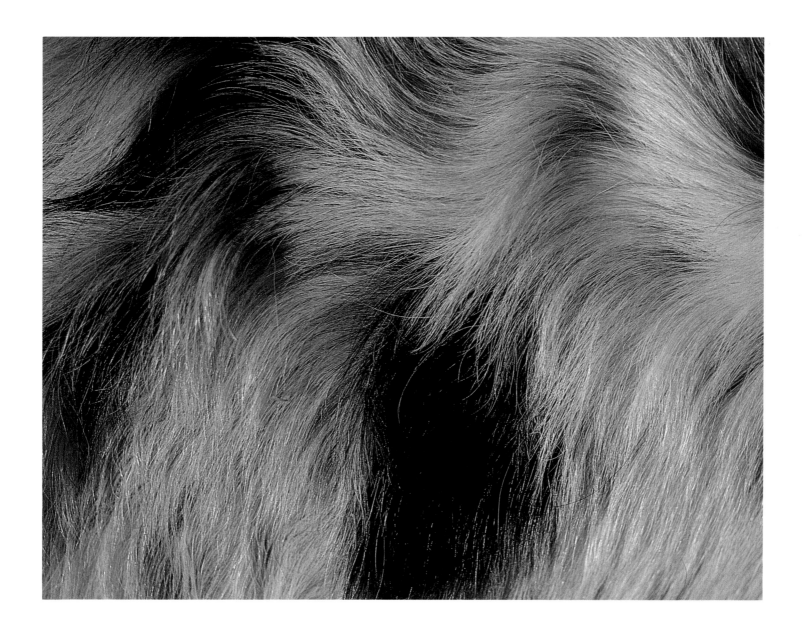

or even raspberries,

or kernels of corn.

No matter where you look, up, down

or all around,

there's always something to see
when you're a nature spy!